YoungNakedSoul

My Confessions

Moonsoulchild

Intro

Before you enter these pages,
I want you to know,
This is every piece of myself
Spilled into these pages.

I want you to know,
This is going to be a wild ride,
So, hold on tight.
A whole insight
Of my soul,
The deepest parts of my heart
You'll feel,
I promise you.

YoungNakedSoul

I dedicate the title
To my dear friend Josie,
Who got called home too soon by God.
For the time I knew her
She taught me more than a lot of souls
Who've been in my life forever,
She was a soul-mate connection
An un-matched soul, a beautiful one
She taught me how to be fearless.
I owe it to her for this journey of becoming an author,
I released my first book in her honor
On April 17, 2018, 1 year of her being in spirit.
She motivated me to share
She poured the inspiration out of me,
If it wasn't for her, I would still be lost.
I never met a friend who I didn't feel I needed to save,
But her, roles reversed, she saved me,
By loving me, accepting and believing in me.
Even after life, she kept being my friend.
I chose this title to honor her,
Because of the friend,
The woman, the soul she was.
I want to keep her alive,
Like her soul shines through the moon at night.
She gave me a sign to be fearless with this one,
So, it was only right to use "YoungNakedSoul"
Not only does it express how naked
I'll leave these pages,
Or the soul you'll feel imprinted in each piece.

It means something to me,
To hold honor in the name she chose
The name that held meaning,
Because of her soul.
I know she's proud,
And when you read this collection
You'll see how naked and fearless I've become,
I have grown.

Josephine Rivera

July 13, 1992 – April 17, 2017

Diversity

I see the world as a whole
Not in pieces, not labeled or colored.
I see love, it doesn't matter
The world's preference,
I'm diverse, love for all
My heart connects to one thing, love.
My heart never lied,
It always knew a kind soul
From a dark one.
I always loved everyone for their heart,
The ones who projected hate,
I left them in the dark.
A sick world we live in,
To leave someone behind
For the color of their skin,
Sexual preference or gender.
It takes being taught hate and thinking the differences
Of someone make them less desirable.
To be vulnerable,
Knowing the world may break my heart,
While holding a guard up, I stand tall.
Keep my vulnerable heart loving, that's all.

God

I'm not religious,
I've been to church about three times.
Honestly, I didn't feel it was necessary,
The God I believe in,
Doesn't need me to go to a place to bare my soul.
He's with me everyday
Anytime, any place
I speak, he listens.
I don't nee to be in the place they call his "home"
I don't need to leave my home,
To go and share my pain with many who worship
The God they believe,
We all have a different vision.
I never believed what others projected,
I never appreciated being pressured
To be in a certain religion,
My relationship with God is different.
I've sinned, I asked him for forgiveness
I've prayed countless times,
He was there no matter the time.
I didn't feel the need to leave the place I feel safest,
To go and share my sins with strangers,
While they listen, it didn't feel right.
No one can tell me I'm going to "hell"
Because I don't see "the right way"
I don't let judgments cloud me,
Only God is allowed in to judge me.
The relationship we share is something I hold close,
God knows my love is real.

I take pride in being the best soul I can be,
I sinned, he forgave
I was lost, he directed me
He's the light,
He brought me the love of my life
After the disaster of my life.
I don't question his decisions for my destiny,
I pray
I thank
I love
I'm a work in progress,
My soul is always searching.
God, always got me,
I'm blessed.

Premenstrual Dysphoric Disorder

I experience depression,
Before it's time for you to arrive
The week before, I get
Upset, flustered, anxious
I'm not myself,
I cry on demand, my moods shift
Like a volcano I explode
I can't control my emotions,
My hormones are out of place.
I fear this time every month,
I fear falling into the same pattern, uncontrollable
I try to take the wheel and steer clear,
Yet, always end up,
Lonely, confused, misunderstood.
Doctors don't understand, "I'm young" they say.
The older I get, it's like my hormones take me to war,
I fight but they always take the best of me.
I'd rather bleed for the whole month
Than experience being loved yet feel alone,
Depressed without control,
Praying it will pass
Praying I can find natural ways to dispose the feeling.
It's like I'm at war with myself
I keep going, I keep fighting,
I declare, I will always make it through.

When I die

I just hope when I die,
I will be remembered for the soul
I gave to the world.
The heart I bleed, fiercely.
I just hope when I die,
I lived my purpose here on earth
And my words are the only thing left of me
Along with my memory,
While the rest flies away
To be with the ones who've been taken from me.
God please tell me,
you have bigger plans for me,
that I, will live my purpose, and live it well.
I want to die when it's time,
Happy
Loved,
Lastly, remembered as
Moonsoulchild
Sara
The woman who wasn't afraid to be fearless.

My Moon

I suffered from sadness the moment you disappeared,
I haven't felt the same happiness,
Since you've been gone.
You brought a new light into my life,
One that shines bright
And never goes out, you are my moon
I search for you everytime it's out,
I call out to you, in hopes you are there,
Your soul made it's way there, and you hear me.
My soul seems to rest, seeing you shine down,
I feel you, everywhere.
Your soul is so rare,
A friend who promised to always be there,
Even in the clouds, you kept that promise.
Your soul seems stronger since you been gone
I feel the force as it brings us closer.
I feel selfish at times, I wish to feel your touch,
Or your smile, only do I dream of the vision
Of that beautiful sight.
Sometimes,
It's peaceful reminiscing you whole,
Then reality hits,
Knowing you're only in spirit and soul
A beautiful disaster I once couldn't accept,
I have found acceptance in your departure,
One day we will meet again, but for now,
I look up and see you,
I love and feel you,
I live fearlessly because of you.

A New Road

I was once lost,
I had to let go a version of myself
That outgrew me.
I wasn't prepared,
I couldn't study a test that wasn't taught to me
Pain comes before love,
Without pain I couldn't see the real.
I chased for love I never felt
I chased for love that was rare,
An illusion of love I had to let go,
Which brought me here.

Lust

I remember being 16,
In love with the idea of love,
Which is why I fell for you.
You gave me the attention I wanted,
Words that held meaning
Until they didn't when actions came into play,
I was exposed as a fool for loving you.
Being 16 I didn't know the meaning of love,
I only knew the meaning of being let go,
Everyone I had interest in,
Became ghost when I opened my heart, but you
Chose to stick around,
Maybe that's why I held onto you.
You showed signs of love,
Even through the lost time uncounted for,
I still yearned for your love.
After being ghost, you came back
Just to leave without a return date.
I couldn't give myself to anyone,
I waited for you, as you promised, you did what you
could to hold me close,
So, I wouldn't wander
So, I wouldn't love another
You had me fooled
I ignored the red flags
I ignored the universe when the signs presented
You weren't enough for me,
I was good enough to leave this behind.

We shared one special day on the bus,
You became vulnerable, I felt bliss when you spoke
That one moment you were real,
Every other, was a lie.
I grew,
And outgrew you.
I saw you for the fool I once was,
Which made it easy to walk away,
You tried to come back and poison me,
I wasn't going to relapse,
It was years being clean without you.
There wasn't anything I wanted from you,
When I learned who you were,
When I made peace with your absence,
It was surreal of the heart you beheld, one that wasn't
meant to love me.
You needed more than I could give,
I didn't need you to keep interfering the road
Of loving myself.
I thought letting you go would kill me,
It only made me stronger.

Breakthrough

I remember being 19 and wise
When it came to loving you,
Unlike when I was 16, a fool.
I remember the night I waited up for you
To get back from a party,
When you were down to visit me but never spent time.
Your teen years are meant to party,
The first sign I overlooked being an old soul
Without a care to waste my life,
Doing drugs
Sleep deprived
A joke.
You were addicted to the fast life,
I was addicted to you.
I was fixated on making you feel my love,
How strong it was, but it wasn't enough to change you,
I should have loved you for who you were
But your character was always in question,
When you came to my house high off molly
Without a care in the world,
5 A.M. pouring your heart out.
You had to get high to express to me,
I couldn't comprehend why you didn't choose
To get high off me,
I never felt like I was enough for you.

In that moment,
You showed your soul, lost and dark.

In that moment,
I knew you weren't for me,
I knew I chased a fool and become one too.
I didn't love you,
I didn't get the chance,
I only loved the idea.
There was no passion,
I was 19,
I wanted to be loved,
I wanted to feel something
I never felt.
I searched for love I never touched,
It may look like the worst mistake,
But your shitty ways taught me,
To never stay where I'm not appreciated
To never turn cold,
When it comes to a questionable heart.

You taught me to love surpassed the pain,
Someone will feel it,
It just wasn't meant to be you.

Lost Time

My heart hurts,
Its exhausted going in circles,
Trying to forget the pain brought to me from losing you.
The pain that remains unspoken,
No words left to speak,
The pain cuts deep.
I loved you,
But couldn't tell you
Because God told you first.

Broken

I broke the moment I heard the news,
You were gone.
I broke,
The moment I felt your soul
And not your touch.
I still yearn for you to be whole.

Anxiety

I try to escape,
I try to write it off,
Once I'm in I can't get out
I overthink, I stress
My heart beats out of my chest,
I fear what comes next,
I can't catch my breath,
I can't reach the other end.
I'm stuck, I'm trapped
Every panic attack I'm left exhausted.
Life always throws me something,
Karma comes in to take what's owed.
I made mistakes, I'm still learning,
I try to breathe but no oxygen left.
Presence of loved ones give me temporary strength,
Once they're gone, I'm left weak.
My mind repeats, it doesn't let me forget
I try to find solutions to the problems I created,
When they finally surface.
A battle I'll always fight,
A silent battle until brought to light,
I can't hide,
Only limit the next time anxiety comes to haunt me
It's disastrous,
So, please be patient.

Michael

The man of my heart,
I can't stop thinking of what we've become,
How strong we have always been.
I look back to my past,
I remember the times I intentionally searched for love,
But you,
I wasn't searching,
I made a friend in you,
I opened my whole life to you,
Secrets and all,
Everything is safe with you.
You are the love of everything
I've done right that I've done wrong.
We created a friendship
We created a foundation
Love grew, our souls, they knew.
We made a home in each other,
We've settled down, together.
No one before can compare,
No love will come after,
We will grow together, stronger
If we continue to be open, honest and true to ourselves.
You are my best friend, my entire world
I love you with my whole heart,
You can keep it, I don't want it back
It's magic being tangled with you,
I never felt love so free, so superhuman
It's you, it will always be you.

*"Some are ungrateful
no matter what I've done for them,
the moment I couldn't do the same, they fold.
I'm sorry, that's not love,
That's convenience."*

*"Just because you brought me pain,
I don't wish the same for you.
I don't want the same karma
coming for me that's coming for you."*

"Where I was isn't where I am,
Or where I'm headed.
If you don't bring inspiration and growth
Along with you,
I will end up outgrowing you."

"There comes a time,
You need to stop guarding your heart
And start letting it guide you."

"Do me a favor,
Stay away from me,
If you don't have good intentions.
I don't have it in me, any longer,
To give my love to those who only abuse it."

"I let them go to save me,
But the loss I felt when I set them free,
Disguised as loss,
But was really a gain.
After all the misery,
I found myself,
The self I drowned in pain."

"I don't crave another presence,
At this moment,
I crave a peace of mind."

"The scars from pain are forever,
The good part about scars,
They always remind you how far you've come."

*"Some people can't handle the truth
when it's spoken,
doesn't mean I'll hold my tongue."*

Mantra:

> *"I won't settle,*
> *For being anyone's convenience,*
> *Just because I'm lonely."*

"I've been poisoned many times,
But no poison was strong enough to kill me."

"I envy people with cold tendencies,
I wish I could separate my heart from feeling.
It's difficult,
When the person my heart yearns for,
Is a perfect example of my soul's match.
It's hard to grasp,
How someone can be a perfect fit
Yet see right through you."

"I always pray for you.
I always pray for I.
I always pray for our love."

"I feel strongly when it comes to my heart,
How deep I love,
How far I'd go to prove it.
I lost myself trying to make love work,
Misunderstood to why it wasn't enough,
Why I wasn't felt.
I was vulnerable,
How much I had to prove meant more than it
being reciprocated."

"My heart beats hard,
It could make some uncomfortable,
My heart longed for more,
Some couldn't reciprocate.
My heart needed balance, security
And it's twin,
Ones from my past were a reflection
Of the love I needed to let go of."

Racism

I don't know what it's like,
To live outside of being white,
I don't know what's like,
To be Black
To be Hispanic
To be Asian
All the different cultures I can't relate to,
We're separated by the color of our skin.
I can't understand the struggles
Of living on this earth not being white,
My heart hurts, because I,
Love everyone equally,
No skin color makes me love you less,
I know it doesn't discard what this world has become
Or the advantage I have over many being white,
I know wishing the world was different
Doesn't change the system,
How the police are corrupted when it comes
To the black man, they take a life,
But let the white man go who was
A murderer
A rapist
An abuser,
When the black man was wrongly accused,
The media won't admit,
Instead,
They let us live in a world filled with racist jerks
Who believe they have an advantage to,
Bully, speak, even kill because of someone's skin color.

My heart breaks to be white in this world
My heart breaks because I can't make it right,
The government has a way of keeping racism alive,
Like it never left, killing all the legends,
Who brought us change,
Martin Luther King Jr.
A man who saw one,
A man who wanted us to share love, as one,
He made it so we could see past color,
We made it this far.

I didn't grow up around racism in my household,
I wasn't taught hate,
I was taught love,
I was taught respect,
I saw color, but I didn't overlook, I saw love.
I never judged or tried to understand, I did listen,
I did educate myself,
I'm still learning.
I know I may never know what it's like,
To live outside of the privilege of being white,
I'm ashamed it has come to that,
I don't wish to be invisible
I don't wish to have privileges,
I only want what's come of me,
No write off's. no shortcuts,
I want equal rights
I want the world to make the change we set out to,
Where we stop separating and come together as one,
I only pray,
The racists can open their eyes.
I only pray,
Racism will die.

Outgrown Friend

You thought pushing me away,
Would always bring me back,
Even closer than before.
Everytime you hurt me,
I saved us,
I held what was left together,
What was left to save,
I was our strength when you chose to destroy us,
Because well,
Your pride shined brighter than our love.
I remember being teens,
The parties
The sleepovers
The boys,
We were best friends,
Until we grew in our 20's,
Our lives took different roads,
I still held our friendship close through our growth.
You demanded more when I was no longer yours,
I broke out my shell and belonged to the world,
When I was discovering,
You made it hard,
Your selfishness broke us,
I couldn't pick up the pieces this time,
I didn't have the strength,
To keep fixing what you kept damaging.
You didn't leave a care behind,
When you put me on a pedestal to the world,
As the bad guy, while you were a saint.
I couldn't undo the damage you done,

I couldn't save what was lost,
You came in like a tornado and blew away
The love that was left,
When you lied on me
When you tried to place your insecurities onto me.
I couldn't teach you to love yourself,
I couldn't even love myself.
I'm sorry our love became tainted,
From all the lies you told only to make you feel whole.
I know you're out there now,
Wondering why we didn't make it.
I know you're wondering why I chose to ghost you,
Without letting you know I loved you,
But I couldn't let you hold that with you,
The power to break me.
After years of being without you,
I still miss you.
I still pray for you, and love you,
It's just, my love took a new direction,
The kind of love in letting you go.

Love Gone Wrong

I loved the idea of you more than I loved you,
As time passed,
I grew to love you.
I overlooked the many times you did me wrong,
The many times you took my love for granted
And chose to shut me out,
When you chose to love me,
When it was convenient for you mental health.
I didn't deserve to be ignored because of your bad day,
I didn't deserve to be treated like I was a burden,
Because you couldn't find your worth along the way.
I'm sorry I never conditioned our love,
I thought I was a superhero,
I thought saving you meant I loved you.
I'm sorry you decided to love me,
When I walked away,
I got lost trying to help you discover you,
I lost the path of my own worth.
You couldn't stand I had the power to be someone,
Because you yet didn't,
I'm sorry you haven't discovered who that may be,
But I'm not sorry for choosing the road which brought
me to leaving you.
I know you'll never understand,
You never felt me the way I needed you to,
So, when you're thinking of me,
Take a moment to realize,
If you loved me,
You wouldn't have made it all about you.

Miscommunication

You say,
I broke your heart,
But you,
Almost broke mine,
Everytime you chose to push me in the dark.
You cant play the blame game,
When your sins came to light,
You chose to deny and not apologize.
You say you're hurt,
Because I walked away,
But you,
Shouldn't have decided to love me,
When time ran out and I was already gone.

Lessons

I left behind our love in the dark,
Like you left me,
I know two wrongs don't make a right,
But I,
Got tired of playing by the rules,
Letting you tear me a part,
So, you could feel strength,
Except the strength you held almost broke me.
You chose to use me to make you feel good,
When you used my insecurities as bait,
To make me love you,
Because you knew if I couldn't love myself,
I wouldn't leave you.
You tricked me into believing you loved me,
When you broke me down, to love yourself,
I couldn't resolve,
Your insecurities had nothing to do with me,
I wish you could have taken a step back to see,
I wish you would have,
Made peace with your past before giving me a chance.
I'm sorry I couldn't save you.

I loved you as the lost soul you were,
The lost soul I tried to help discover,
The worth you kept running from,
I couldn't be your savior.
I'm not sorry I had the strength to walk away,
When times became dark,
I couldn't bring the light any longer,
I couldn't make you see when you wished I could,
I'm not a genie,

I couldn't grant you the wishes,
You wished to come true,
I'm only human, with a heart that loved you,
With every piece I could,
Until you came in like a wrecking ball
And shattered us into pieces.

I wanted to apologize for leaving you,
When your mental health was in question,
But mine,
Was in question too.
I chose myself,
After choosing you,
So, I'm not sorry.
I pray you're out there,
Trying to find yourself too.
I'm most grateful,
Because you lead me to happiness,
I pray you see it was best to let you free,
There wasn't happiness in we.

Nature

The beach at night,
Watching the sun go down,
And the moon come out,
Shine over the ocean,
Listening to the waves speak,
My soul feels at peace.
One of my favorite places
One of my last moments I shared with you.

June 23, 2018

I will forever be thankful you were there and helped
me survive the storm.

July 5, 2018

Whether we become one,
One day,
I still have the greatest memories of my life.
I thank you,
For giving me the chance,
To love you,
To experience a piece of life with you
You have become my best friend,
I hope you know that.

Death

It's the scariest thing in the world,
To know your loved ones
will one day disappear from earth.
Their spirit will fly high into another world,
Yet follow and keep us safe.
We choose to be selfish,
Ask them to still be here without understanding,
They're still living.
Guilt becomes one of the biggest feelings,
We say things we didn't once mean,
Things we can't take back.
I lost many to God,
I cried tears until I've had none left,
I was left confused,
How could it be possible to live without them?
My heart couldn't rest without their love.
How was it possible to live on,
Without being whole?
I was selfish when it came to wanting them back,
I couldn't grasp the concept of never seeing them.

I lost a close friend,
It brought me to the darkest parts of my soul
I never knew existed,
I became sick from the anxiety,
Many thoughts ran through my mind,
It didn't make any sense,
Until God make sense of the mess.
The signs from her,

How she worked overtime to show her existence
wasn't diminished,
The love she brought,
The light,
How my life hasn't been great,
Sometimes I feel wrong to feel that way,
That I should soak in my sorrows,
But she brought a new sense of purpose.
I slowly accepted death as a part of life even though it
scared the shit out of me,
I have balance and understanding,
After death there's life,
Even stronger than before.
Soul's don't die, bodies do
The spirit that lives on is what should be focused on,
That's the love we knew.

Loving an Addict

They say,
Addiction is a disease,
I say it's a choice,
I know many people will disagree,
But I'm not up for discussion,
I'm asking you to just listen.
Addiction tore my family apart,
I watched someone I loved, lose themselves,
They chose to shoot up with no regret,
That's how I saw it.
I was left in despair,
To think they cared more about their drug of choice
Than to ask for a helping hand,
I couldn't grasp the emptiness they felt,
I was there, many of us were,
Except we weren't enough,
When their drug of choice was.
A lot focus only on the addict and not the impacted,
Why do many call it a disease?
Because it can kill you? There's no cure?
No one ever had a valid argument,
I don't care if science says it's a disease,
I refuse to believe,
No one is an addict until they chose to be,
When they first choose to try,
To find an escape, a temporary fix,
Slowly killing themselves not to feel a thing,
To me, that's dead,
Its selfish.

Choosing the easy way,
While you hurt everyone down your path,
Steal to pawn for your next fix,
Items that can't be replaced, that held meaning,
I know material things don't hold high value,
But when it's all you have left of someone,
It holds more value than the world.
It hurts to be,
Betrayed
Lied too
Played as the fool,
After being told "I'm trying" without a change.

Addiction is more than the disease you speak,
It's more than a good time that turns into a dark one,
It's a battlefield that breaks everyone involved.
I never had the desire to pick up and shoot up,
So, I can't tell you what it feels like,
Whether it's the greatest feeling,
I can tell you what it's like to love an addict,
It's one of the most damaging life experiences,
There are no words to express,
The feelings surfaced the moment you hear the news.

I never saw it as a disease,
It wasn't fair to those with cancer without control.
It's not fair to compare a bad decision,
To months to live.
Yes, addiction kills,
You chose to intoxicate your body,
You knew the damage it would make.
Saying it's a disease,
Helps addicts justify why,

Saying it's a disease makes it seem "okay"
It makes an excuse for each relapse.

I have high hopes for people,
There's more to someone than the demons they fight,
It was a long journey of,
Broken hearts
Broken Families
Loneliness
Unforgeable memories.
We're here,
We've forgiven,
We've moved on, recovered.
It comes down to strength,
To decide there's more important things to sacrifice
than yourself,
Family sticks together,
Even through a broke home,
There's still time to pick up the pieces,
It's your choice.

Absent Parent

I was 13 the last time I saw my father,
He left without a goodbye,
He left without a reason,
Left me without the closure I needed,
Left me without the love I needed,
Until I grew to realize I didn't need it.
My parents were never married,
They broke up while I was young,
It was just my mom and my sister until my step-father
came into the picture,
I was confused
I would wonder,
Who's to blame, or if there was anyone to blame,
Finally, I gave up,
It hurt to be ghosted by someone I loved,
My own father couldn't be a man and step up,
Be the father he should've been,
Watching my mother doing it all while my
grandparents helped,
I'm so grateful to have the love expressed from
everyone, it made the void smaller,
But when I was alone,
I found myself at a crossroad,
How could someone leave without reason,
Completely disappear from my life and only live 15
minutes away?
When I saw him years later at the store,
He looked at me, more like, through me,
Didn't recognize me,
Which is crazy being his twin.

He couldn't see the love that was lost,
A love I held in my heart for who I wished he could be,
The one who ran off with a piece of me.
He missed the big achievements of my life.
People would say "a least you have a step-father"
I'm blessed to have someone walk in,
When he walked out,
It's a void that can't be redone,
It's not the same,
We all have hopes, our parents stay happy and we don't end up in a broken home,
As I watched my mother love a man who treated her right, I understood I needed to be kinder,
And accept my fate.
I grew to love my step-father,
He taught me structure
He taught me disciple,
I give many thanks to my mother and him,
For raising me to be a beautiful human,
A woman of honor and dignity,
I'm most grateful,
To have someone pick up the pieces,
Who stepped in when he didn't have to,
Loved me when he didn't have to.
I'm now 26,
My father re-entered my life without explanation why he left.
I learned to accept there's still time,
He doesn't know how lost I was, nor will he,
He doesn't deserve to hold my pain,
I'm proud to say I made it through his absence without being broken, so truly, nothing can break me.

A Letter to My Ex,

I set aside the pain, heartache, and misery to write this. I took everything into consideration to finally leave this behind. I hid a lot of my hurt so only I could see, no one felt my pain because I didn't choose to display it, I didn't feel the need to paint you as the picture you deserved, I gave you more credit than you deserved. I set aside the pain you brought me and kept the love for you alive, because my heart never did wrong until you chose to overlook me, until you chose to pollute me with your toxicity. It may seem naïve to put you on display as the bad guy, and I, take no blame, but I've made peace with my involvement in the hurt I brought too, I took accountability for the pain I intentionally placed onto you, but you deserved it, I'm not sorry. I'd be lying if I said I was. I made an oath to never lessen my worth to make myself available for you, or anyone else's standards. I learned my lesson I was meant to, even if it wasn't planned, I learned from my mistakes. Apologizing isn't something I plan to do, I didn't do anything I regret, I didn't tear your heart a part like you did mine, the way things ended was fair, it's how you chose to play, I just defended my ground. You gave me shit for walking away, I gave you shit for the years you were blind, how could you not appreciate my heart, or even, my existence? I didn't waste a moment, every moment spent was meant to be. The love I felt was strong and real, my heartbeat was for you and only you. Unfortunately, the love never happened to get reciprocated the same, and I, never left because my heart chose you more times than I could have a say, because I, never let love go when I felt safe. You never physically hurt me, you never put me in danger, in that aspect, I felt safe. I was trapped in your social anxiety. I became scared of society. We lived behind the scenes, we barely experienced life, you were too cared, I became accustomed to your ways, me being shy in my past, you brought out my lifeless ways.

I thought what we had was special, spending all our off time together, I loved your family, as you only met mine twice, I was secluded from the life I once knew to be yours. I gave up friendships for you. I got into the dark side with people I loved, because I always chose you. I was blind. I was a fool. Above all, I chose love, more so, what felt like love to me, because I, never felt the kind of love you brought over me. Our honeymoon phase lifted not too long after we fell, but I stayed because I thought we'd make it through, I was convinced you were all I'd ever needed. I searched for someone to love me for years, so you're damn right I held on for dear life when it came to you. I gave you time to prove there was more than what presented. I tried to take our lives to the next level, but you chose to stand still, afraid to move forward. The day I chose to walk away you saw me for everything I am, even though you'll never admit it, I know you're aware of the heart I have that never changed. I know there's a lot you won't admit and choose to hold inside while you put me on a pedestal to the world as the one who broke you, but listen, our history goes back too far for you to blame me for the disaster that became us. I took my blame, it's time for you to take blame, too. It's time for you to open your eyes and see the hurt I brought was because I wasn't being felt or heard. Of course, you opened your eyes when I confided in someone else, your heart broke. You had time to save us, my heart was big enough to hear you out, but you chose to tear me down every chance you could with your words. Your truth spoke the many times you opened your mouth, your tears didn't change a thing, all I saw was guilt all over your face. You thought I was leaving you for someone else, you thought I planned this, but the only person I was leaving you for was myself. I lost myself within you. I lost every part of who I wanted to be when I became a part of you. Yes, we had some good times, but truthfully, our bad days overplayed way too many times to remember the good. I was sad far too many times, I was far from happiness to even know what it felt like. I was desperate to leave. I just didn't have what it took to hurt you. That's the difference between you and I, even after everything you put me through, I still tried to save you from the suffering, but you, were like a wrecking ball, continuously hurting me like it was something rewarding, as I stayed, you didn't see the wrong in your ways, you couldn't hear my side, you couldn't feel my pain, if that wasn't reason enough to leave you, tell me, what else was I supposed to do?

Marriage

I never believed in marriage,
I grew up in a broke home,
Two parents that didn't make it together,
One who didn't make it alone.
One thing I did,
Was grow up surrounded by love,
Marriage wasn't on my mind,
I never dreamt of the perfect wedding,
I dreamt of the perfect love,
I grew up learning marriages ended more than they lasted,
I saw it as a piece of paper,
A big expense if it ended.
I grew up watching love be more important
Than rushing into signing a certificate.
My mother and step-father have been together since I was 12, they aren't married.
I never fantasized the wedding because I never saw the importance when being faithful and in love,
Overpowered the bond that was always there,
I thought that's what mattered,
Not stepping out on your partner.
Being a team
Being a friend
Loving unconditionally,
I had the right ideas of love,
Seeing people jump into marriages,
Thinking it will keep their partner,
Or having a child,
Are the wrong decisions to tie the knot.
Can you blame me for running from the idea?

Not caring to spend thousands of dollars on ONE special day?
A dress I'll wear once,
People I don't even want there just for gifts,
Family drama once the liquor hits,
I'm sorry, but I, never dreamt of this,
Doesn't mean I didn't dream of love.
I don't associate love with marriage,
I always associated it with lust,
Everyone I've known always did it for the thrill, or never had a deeper meaning, or ended too soon,
I'm not to blame,
Society is,
For the claim of what marriage and love is,
Neither are the same,
Not this day in age.
I never lost hope of love,
Through the disaster of marriage,
I kept searching, dreaming, hoping,
It all paid off,
I found my love,
There's no question whether I'd marry him,
On the right terms,
When the time is right,
Because our love is timeless.
The day it happens,
All the fancy traditions will be thrown out the window,
We'll create our own,
I don't live up to society's standards,
No one can tell me what love I,
I already know.

Loneliness

When I think of loneliness,
I think of you,
A soul who flew to the clouds way too soon,
You didn't deserve to be taken before your purpose was
presented,
You left so much purpose in my life,
You brought light when it was dark,
Even after you're gone,
You still shine bright,
Like the moon at night,
Your light shines brighter than any star,
They have nothing on you.
I felt loneliness the moment I heard you were gone,
A feeling that hasn't gone away, never will,
A piece of me is with you,
I've learned to manage.
Loneliness is a feeling of emptiness, love, and pain,
All emotions poured into one,
It's feeling lost without direction,
It's going in circles without a destination.
Loneliness became less the moment I felt you,
When I asked God to let me feel you one last time,
In the 100-degree shower, crying uncontrollably,
Asking God to speak with you, to give me a sign,
I felt a cold breeze come through the shower,
I stopped crying and smiled, and knew,
Loneliness became bliss,
The moment I felt you.

The Other Woman

The other woman,
I once was.
I wasn't ashamed,
I had no control over what I didn't know,
I thought I was the only one,
I can take blame for continuing once I knew,
In my defense,
My heart was already invested,
Even though it was based on a lie.
I once was a fool for a man,
Who chose me as his second choice,
While entertaining his first.
I remember getting many signs from her,
To run and find love elsewhere,
I was convinced he loved me.
Was I really to blame, because I was in love with
someone who was good at faking?
Someone who was good at making it seem I was the
only one?
I didn't know what to believe,
I held on to any hope I had left,
To save what wasn't yet ruined.
I kept getting swept off my feet,
By someone who couldn't catch me,
Who watched me yearn for his love,
Used it as his advantage to keep me,
He used my love as his escape,
I was a fool.
After years passed,
She, the other woman, called me,
We spoke for hours,

It was peaceful to hear the truth from all sides,
She told me while he was with me,
She lived with him.
He felt like he needed to be with me,
So, she let him free,
While she stuck around,
In that moment I wasn't angry,
I didn't feel a thing,
We already said our goodbyes,
Hearing her truth didn't alter the story,
I was already disconnected from him.
I learned one thing,
I thought all along I was the fool,
It was her, the other woman,
I prayed for her.

Lies

Lies were told many times,
There's no measure of whether it was big or small,
A lie is a lie,
It hurt,
It almost broke and utterly damaged my soul.
Someone I loved decided to alter the truth,
To "save" me from the pain,
It hurt more disguising the truth to their truth,
They believed it,
The many times they practiced it,
I always imagined being more,
Yet always settling for the lies,
Hoping the lies became truth.
The lies didn't die,
They only became stronger,
Dealing with someone who didn't care
To bare my soul with love that's tainted
Just to keep me around.
My love wa rare,
To lose,
They couldn't bear.
So, they chose to lie to keep me there,
Until I played their game against them,
Watched them drown in regret,
Begging me to forgive,
Said they would never lie again,
I caught them lie again,
The only sight they ever saw of me again,
Was me walking.

My Human

The passion we have for another runs deep,
As deep as our hearts bleed,
Our love makes us invincible,
We bring no pain,
We made peace with our pasts,
We loved ourselves before we loved us.
I was doing it wrong until I got reintroduced to myself,
In a different skin,
One I can see myself in,
The one you helped me find beauty in.
You introduced me to a different side of me I never
knew was there.
Being a friend to you has opened my eyes to the real,
I couldn't unsee what wasn't for me,
I couldn't fake it,
Or turn a blind eye to it.
I was woke, to the illusion I placed upon love,
I was woke, to the love that awakened my soul,
The kind of love I prayed for,
A connection I longed for.
You are the man I dreamt about,
I never thought it could be possible,
For dreams to come true,
Until I woke up and you weren't a dream,
But an angel sent from God,
To love me, hold me, and keep me safe.
I no longer dream, too many times I'd sleep just to feel
you,
You are more than a dream,
You are my soul in human form.

Settled

I settled for the comfort of an unhappy home,
While praying for a fantasy I dreamt of a reality out of reach,
I chose to preach being comfortable,
Without knowing the difference,
Of comfort and being settled,
I convinced myself I was happy because I was comfortable.
The dream was far from reality,
My prayers never got answered,
I stayed, I'm a survivor of what it's like to experience unhappiness for years, without making a change.
The thought of starting over and opening up to another scared me, It was rare when I let someone in.
If I wasn't happy,
I still had the heart to make it work.
I tried creating happiness where it didn't work,
I tried making love exist in people who weren't out to love me.
I'm a good woman, with a heart full of love,
I searched and chased for the match of my soul,
Too many times I lost control,
I took the wheel of many souls but couldn't handle what they had to offer,
I was blinded by the love I wanted to give,
I accepted what they had to offer,
Even if,
It wasn't good,
It wasn't meant for me.
I don't think that makes me a shitty person,
I think it makes me human.

Natural Beauty

It was a struggle,
Trying to love what I covered in makeup,
I was told I looked better with it.
I had trouble fighting the demons I had with my natural
self,
Until I stopped listening to the noise,
Opened my eyes and saw the flaws that made others
uncomfortable,
Are what made me beautiful.

Old Attachments

Being with someone new,
Without holding onto old attachments from past love,
Was a battle.
I projected the wrongs onto the new one,
They didn't deserve to do time for another soul's crime
on my heart,
They didn't bring pain,
So, why would I project past pain onto them?
I created boundaries between my past and what's next,
Once I made peace with what's gone.

No two souls are the same,
I couldn't blame
I couldn't love,
Until I healed from the last,
No one deserved to be with me until I could.

A Non-Physical Fear

Losing the love that keeps my heart beating,
The feeling of love,
The kind of love that projects my soul,
The kind of love I was once scared to show the world.
I wore my heart on my sleeve,
That's not a physical fear, things like,
Heights
Bridges
Dying,
Those are physical.
I fear,
Losing the love that keeps me alive,
Leaving this world without fulfilling my purpose.
I hold more fears that come with being physical, yet
they all come back to dying,
Heights scare me, why would I make myself available
to death, or play with the devil?
I'm meant to stand on my two feet,
Why would I need an adrenaline rush for a couple
seconds of fun,
Kind of like drugs,
They lift you until they break you,
I don't urge the sudden rush.,
But love,
Is the kind of rush I need,
Love is me.

Abortion

I'm not one who has a strong opinion on everything,
On topics that are big or start wars,
I know my opinions can't save the world,
But a least my voice is heard.
Men don't know what it's like,
To carry a child
To birth a child,
They should get to tell a woman to abort or not to.
We as women,
We should have the right not to birth a baby that didn't
come out of love, more so,
In hate,
Without our consent,
We shouldn't have to live with the memory of being
taken advantage of,
It's our body,
We have a right to free ourselves from the pain we
were brought,
We have a right to choose to decide,
We bring a life into this world that wasn't our choice.
Some say,
It doesn't matter if we were raped,
Yet they call this "the land of the free"
Yet set boundaries.
As women,
We should protect ourselves when we're not ready,
Play it safe,

Make sure it doesn't end up a mistake.
When it's out of our control,
We shouldn't be controlled
We should have a voice
We should have a say.
It's our body for the record,
It's our life to raise,
In a broken home,
A trauma filled heart.

We should get to decide,
That's all we want,
To have a voice that's heard,
But unfortunately,
Non-abortion laws,
Rule.

Invisible

I have friends who supported me but never brought a
book,
Some family haven't acknowledged I wrote one.
Here I am,
Baring my soul to the world.
Some might not support because I was once that
broken 9-5 girl,
Come home without purpose.
They see my success as nothing but highlight the times
I was lost,
They see me as less,
They see my art as a hobby,
Until they see the sales and wonder, how?
Without reading a single word,
Some should pick up a book and read,
Might open their eyes to the side they never knew,
Might open their eyes to them through my eyes,
Not everyone's invincible,
Pride and ego are all locals hold close.

The quiet girl now speaking louder,
I grew.
Never thought I'd see the day,
People I don't know clap for me,
While people I love,
Downplay me.
Just remember,
When I make it,
Do me one favor,
Stay ghost.

Uncomfortable Sexual Experience

I was the only virgin alive in my high school,
Or so it seemed.
I had guys who tried to wine and dine me just to try,
But I had plans to wait for the one I loved,
Someone I would spend my life with,
I never gave in,
All my friends were sexually active,
It confused some,
I wasn't but my friends were.
Sex is all everyone wanted and there I was,
A virgin, on top of being the girl who didn't talk,
Can you imagine? A Joke.
I saved myself,
I didn't think it would mean anything without love,
I was 19,
In love, blinded by the words he spoke that held no
actions,
I was in love with a boy who wanted what I was saving.
People ask me,
"How was your first"
It was uncomfortable, I try to forget it often,
I remember telling him to stop,
But he kept going, it was like his time was enjoyable,
until he heard me,
I was blinded by the love,

I didn't see the discomfort until I didn't want to do it again,
I refused the thought of sex.
My first time was taken,
He didn't take the time to explore my mind and body,
He took what he wanted while leaving me scarred years to come.
It was a mess, a wreck,
I felt taken advantage of,
I couldn't trust another with the power to change my mind.
I never defined it as rape because I was blinded by love, until I realized,
This one encounter made every other harder.

Born Without A Voice

I grew up the shy girl,
The girl who never talked,
When anyone saw me, they had to point it out,
It was uncomfortable,
I never spoke up.
I didn't think it was a crime,
People at school played on it like it was,
It was like the world was ending,
Everytime they heard me speak.
They captured my voice,
I saw everyone as they were out to hurt me,
Some bullied, knowing I wouldn't respond,
I hope you know how bad I felt inside when you picked
me a part because I didn't talk to you,
Why didn't you ever think, maybe it was you?
The power of voice, they say,
I say the power of silence.
This is my truth,
For all the ones who thought they broke me,
You made me.
I chose my friends wisely,
I didn't want to be popular,
You can have your high school fame,
I'm living my dream,
A voice you can't silence,
I'm powerful now.
I'm stronger, I don't just have a voice,
I have the means to hurt you,
But my voice is to tell my story,
Not to bully.

2018

You taught me pain,
And with pain comes love.
You taught me change,
And with change comes growth.
You taught me patience,
And with patience comes blessings.
You taught me so much,
You also showed me.

Showed me love
Showed me success
Showed me happiness

I'm most grateful to experience,
A year full of lessons and blessings.
I love you,
I'm not afraid to let you go,
Above all,
You made me fearless.

Love Note

Since you walked into my life,
I haven't wished to see a day without you.
I know,
I can be on my own, and be an independent woman,
Life already dealt me those cards,
I found the love in my solitude.
There's just,
something magical in sharing my heart with you.

Anyone from My Past

I didn't need you to feel confident
I didn't need you to become the woman I am,
Unfortunately,
The pain that came from being tied to you helped me
discover who I am.
Now, before you go saying you made me,
Make sure you mention you're the lost one.

The First Time

I always think back to the first time I felt love,
The confusion of whether it was,
Or just lust.
I was the only one who kept us alive,
While you,
Were so good at destroying every hope I kept alive.

Ghost

After all the "I miss you" attached to no actions,
After all the ghosting and returning,
I'm not a convenience,
I'm a priority.
I have this terrible habit of cutting people out my life
without speaking to them again,
In my dense,
I wouldn't of chose this,
They led me to it.

Grow

I never hurt anyone the way they hurt me,
Until they decided to show me,
I was worthless.
I never chose to walk away,
Until they showed me which direction to take,
I didn't see the door until they pushed me towards it.
When I open myself to someone, I give everything,
How do you love in half?
I made it possible to be broken,
I don't regret the love I gave,
I know I only did right by everyone I loved,
And let love me.
I know you feel I left you,
I chose to love my instead,
I couldn't love you as I promised,
I gave you everything I had, in the moment we shared.
What I gave,
Wasn't meant to stay as long, as I promised,
We grew,
I grew.
Not everyone love stays a fire,
Some are only meant to be a flame,
I will outgrow what's meant to outgrow me,
That doesn't make me a burden.

Real Love

It's incredible,
To witness real love after the illusion I placed on it.
It's beautiful,
Falling without realizing I was deep in,
Without the chase or trying to prove my love.

A love that's conditioned with foundation.
A love of friends before our heart's took over.

Sometimes

Sometimes I need to hurt,
To understand what's not meant for me.
Sometimes I'm stubborn and choose,
Not to go down a road of destruction,
Knowing it will bring pain,
Without acknowledging,
It will bring me through.

User

Everyone needs me when they need something,
Or going through it,
I'm happy to be at your need while you're going through
tragedy, but I,
Also like to experience the parts that are beautiful.
Except I'm not needed,
So, they ghost me until they need me again.

Vows

I won't ever let a love like ours go,
Or die,
I will live in, nourish it, cherish it,
Forever keep it alive.
For once,
I feel alive,
I owe that to you.
I'm whole from the love I give myself,
And that missing piece,
The one that fits with you.

Blessing

I've prayed to be where I am,
Physically, mentally, emotionally,
Every part of being is healthy, happy, and loved.
I'm taking care of me, my heart, my happiness,
I'm taken care of.
I love myself enough to love another,
That's my blessing.

"I started loving myself more,
When I stopped loving you.
I found myself,
When I stopped trying to make you understand."

"I heard stories about love,
A lot ended with,
"because I loved them"
It's terrifying to know,
Some have this image of love,
so heartbreaking,
All because,
they kept loving someone wrong for them."

"Love is like a rollercoaster,
It looks fun,
But when you're on it,
It can be scary and dangerous,
That's the risk I took loving you."

No Desire Being Friends with Exes

I chased, I let my heart become a weapon against me. I didn't set boundaries, I refused to see the red flags, I always created love even when it wasn't healthy. I went in the direction I thought was love, or where love could grow. I confused lust with love many times, I couldn't get passed, "everything happens for a reason" just to let someone go. I held on even when the signs were against me. Words were spoken, I never listened. I loved hard. One thing I never could grasp, the meaning of loving and letting go. I had to show I loved hard. The chase, the race of trying to make someone see my love was exhausting, but I felt relieved when I could make them love me. I felt like a superhero when I saved them from their pain, I proved my love could heal them. After all the chasing and saving, we're at the finish line sharing this moment of "love" I created, it doesn't feel as good as I imagined. When love vanished, comfort took it's place, it became routine. I didn't know my purpose, or what I wanted from a relationship other than being loved. I couldn't tell you what I loved about myself, I couldn't condition any love. I held pain in my heart, I also brought it. My karma was to feel pain and relief at the same time. I ended up unfulfilled because I had no purpose, I already replayed everything I had to offer. I convinced myself there was love but it never felt enough. I always had good intentions and followed with a heavy heart, I also walked away, ghosted, and brought the same heartache I felt. I didn't bring pain because I was malicious, or because I didn't love them, I was no longer happy. When my purpose in their lives were no longer needed, I stayed longer than I was welcomed. It became toxic, our love became tainted, we became lost. It's normal to hurt someone without the intention, I never meant to bring heartache to anyone I loved, even though I never conditioned the love, the love that grew still left meaning on my heart. I became toxic to myself keeping myself away from growing in the direction without ones I loved. Having a big heart almost broke me, it built me. The version of myself I couldn't have found without the pain. It took a lot of patience. Letting go didn't mean I never loved them, I just decided not to drown when it came to choose.

I'm not sorry I chose me.

I pray you don't hold me in vain, and one day pray for me too.

Followed My Heart, Not the Opinions

I don't care what someone thought,
I'd still ask for their opinion,
Open my mind to the unknown,
A different vision,
In case I was blind for some reason.
When it's something I want, and my intuition backs me
up, I do what I wanted,
The opinion's don't mean anything more,
Regardless of how much I love you.
Before meeting Michael,
We were 1,200 miles apart,
I lived in Connecticut, he lived in Florida,
We met on Twitter,
Two authors living the same dream,
Friendship built,
A real connection grew from the foundation we set.
It was confusing for some,
Because "how" was the question,
We lived 24 hours away driving, a 3-hour plane ride.
I had people I loved telling me I shouldn't,
I didn't know him,
Was their reflection looking in,
They didn't know we've been learning each other,
Or how he helped me feel safe through the chaos of my
present life,
When it was chasing down,

He held me high.
When feelings sparked, I needed to know,
So, I chose to go,
I never felt a fire so strong,
One that knocked out every fear in my body,
I chose to get on a plane for the first time alone to meet him,
The opinions weren't transparent,
"You don't know him"
"You never flew alone"
I listened, I respected their opinions,
My whole being chose to go against their wishes,
They separated their opinions from the situation,
They wanted to best for me,
So, they let me free.
I was fearless the day I left,
I had to,
If I didn't,
I wouldn't be with you.

Goodbyes

I'm not good at goodbyes,
I never was,
I'd rather disappear like a ghost than confront the pain,
I couldn't put that pain on my heart even if it was my
fault, even if it was me who was consumed by toxicity.
Once I became attached,
I couldn't let go.
Goodbyes were something I didn't learn,
I was accustomed to loving until it hurt.
Goodbyes didn't always bring pain,
They brought closure,
A new sense of purpose,
Moving on didn't bring that heart aching pain I once
knew,
They brought peace,
The kind I couldn't have with them.

"It's hard being an artist working a 9-5,
No job ever feels satisfying,
No job makes me happy,
I want to create all times of the day,
But the pressure of being stressed by
miserable people,
Being underpaid,
Always gets the best of me.

I want to be free."

Love Note

When I fell for you, I wasn't searching for love, I was searching for peace. I was searching for a friend. You were the light within my darkness, the calm to my anxious nerves. When I fell, I fell in love with the person you are, the loving, kind, beautiful soul you are. I fell in love with the man you're growing into every day, every day I fall more, I look into your eyes and wonder how I lived my whole life not knowing who you were. I was searching for you in everyone I ever loved. The way I love you can't be compared to past loves, you put them all to shame. You walked into my life t the perfect moment, I prayed to find you sooner, I searched for you in every lover I tried to define, everyone I tried to make love me. I wasn't ready for your back then, I had to know what love didn't feel like. I had to know what damaged felt like, to know my worth was more important than letting anyone else break me down. I went through several "wrong one's" to be prepared for your love. I had to grow as a woman to be set to give you the love you deserved, I never wanted to hurt you. If I was to meet you sooner, I probably would have. I was healing. Loving someone else when I couldn't figure myself would be a mess. I fell in love with your willingness to be open with me, your unconditional friendship. Falling in love with you was something I never saw coming, I think that's what makes our love special, it chose us. Our love is the kind people hope to find one day. God gave me you, that's why I know I deserve this love.

Cheating

I've heard people say,
"Cheating is a character thing"
"Once a cheater, always a cheater"
I hold that to the highest of wrongs,
Because I,
Cheated once, but never again,
I learned my lesson,
I don't regret doing it, I felt he deserved it,
I was in a circle of confusion,
Hoping he'd never find out, yet wishing he would,
So, he would let me free,
I wasn't strong enough to leave,
I didn't feel there was more for me than him,
I was accustomed to his life,
I lost all direction of myself when I chose to let him
take control,
I built up anger from all the dirt he kept in the dark
that brought to light,
All those times his ex, contacted him to rekindle the
toxicity they shared, to fuck, maybe love one more
time, just to break him again.
He never gave in but sure flirted the idea.
He downplayed me to a random mistress,
Told her I was only attractive online,
My heart broke,
I didn't tell a single soul,
I just happened to find someone interested in giving me
a moment, we shared a moment, I felt no regret.
The sex was a rush until I felt my soul crush.
I realized how much hurt I could bring if he ever knew.

I thought I could erase the pain,
The moment was only great in the time it happened,
Until I returned to my life,
Where lies were told,
I loved a man who couldn't love my natural,
He said what he could,
To get in the pants of another,
I felt cheated in that moment,
I reacted without thinking the pain it would leave me,
I justified it as he deserved it,
He had no clue I had the power to destroy him,
I stayed silent about my mistake.
For 3 years,
He never knew about my sin,
He never could admit to what he said,
The day I left, he apologized,
It was too late,
Our relationship was based off lies.
I tried to make it work without cheating again,
His dirt never stopped,
I know two wrongs don't make a right,
But in the moment,
I didn't know the purpose,
I just wanted to feel justified
I just wanted to feel stronger.

Stuck

We had good times, we laughed,
He had a great family,
Only thing missing was the passion,
We barely had sex,
I thought it was boring,
Our relationship felt more like a friendship,
The beginning held the most meaning until we grew,
I learned his true colors,
It wasn't fun trying to love someone who was
interested in other woman,
He opened my eyes to explore women,
Something I always wanted to, but was scared, the
time wasn't right, people loved to judge.
I grew fearless the more I lived,
I wasn't afraid to show myself publicly,
To be with a woman was different,
I enjoyed it,
So, I thank him for opening what I hid deep inside me.
It was overplayed,
Trying to have threesomes I didn't desire to be in,
The ones we did I enjoyed the women more.
Our relationship became boring,
No attention placed onto me,
His attention was on the next,
Trying to find another woman, it was exhausting,
Trying to get him to be interested in what I had to offer,
Someone who was infatuated with multiple women,
But couldn't be pleased by me.

I felt threatened by the many times I saw him speaking to his ex,
As he promised he wouldn't, the universe always aligned, the signs always came on time.
I stayed quiet, because when I spoke, I always got the run around, I was always made out to be crazy.
Looking back,
I don't know why I didn't run, but it's hard seeing the mess when I was trapped in it.
I became toxic dealing with someone so cold, but also showed me happiness in the darkest way,
I felt safe in the moment,
For once someone loved me back.
I didn't want to give it all up because of the insecurities I felt, from past loves coming to visit,
Trying to get back where heart's broke.
I thought the love we shared was something real,
What we shared was convenient,
We were both searching for help to repair our hearts,
I fixed him,
He almost broke me.
I thought I'd hurt from losing all I built,
I didn't feel a thing.

"Communication is important in all stages of life,
But your 20's,
Your growing era, it's vital.
These days,
If you can't come to me and communicate any
issue or concern,
I'm leaving you behind.

I don't have time to fix, or save
Anything I didn't ruin."

"Silence is powerful,
It's a language understood
without speaking a word."

"I never changed my love language,
My heart remained the same,
Pain didn't change me."

You don't have to understand when it comes to my mental health, you can either get educated, or don't open your mouth.

I have unbearable social anxiety. I didn't find my voice until after high school. I spoke to who I felt comfortable with, which made it hard to let go of people. I hate big crowds. I despise public speaking. I would always plan a conversation in my head beforehand–how would I look? I was concerned with my public imagine, I thought if I didn't speak, I wouldn't be noticed, unfortunately, it brought the opposite.

I weighted 90-100 until about 22, it was the first thing people said upon meeting me, it was like they never saw someone skinny, exaggerating it to "do you even eat" very unpleasant. I never understood why it mattered to anyone.

I thought never speaking a word, meant no one had anything to speak of me spiritually, instead they chose to speak on my image. No one ever thought to care about my mental health when they decided to joke about my weight, or how it would affect me once they kept replaying the same storyline, making me more of an outcast.

I'm a worrier, I tent to overthink everything. Anxiety gets the best of me more than I can control. I've once been consumed by my peers, now, I'm learning to silence the noise.

God Sent

I couldn't have prayed harder to have my prayers answered. It took God sometime to prepare this love. It took God some time to make it right before we found each other, the timing was perfect, everything about us is unbreakable.

You match my energy.

You match my weirdness.

You match my sex drive.

You match my heart.

You're my twin flame, when I stare into your eyes, I find myself gazing into the dream I once kept following into, except we're more than a dream. What you give to me is something I can't find in someone else. Your love is the kind of love I tried to make work within every lover I beheld in my heart, just to end up disappointed.

God knew I wasn't ready back then, he knew I had to find who I was, to love myself, before I could love you.

"I let go of people I still love,
That's strength, that's growth."

*"Love me while I'm here,
I deserve it."*

Overcoming the Storm

The storm,
After every panic attack,
I fell deep into my mind,
I let it play tricks on me,
I found myself in the darkness with no way out,
No one to run to,
If someone's there,
Their presence is temporary.
The storm didn't let up,
Because of a couple moments of happiness,
They disappear once I'm alone,
My minds flooded,
My heart's broken,
I felt stuck,
I felt weak.
I never made it passed the storm,
I always lived it until I overcame it,
I watched it almost kill me,
Until I took control–
Death
Losing loved ones
Outgrowing
Letting free
Change,
These are my biggest lessons,
I feared facing and feeling, and what came next,
Until I found peace in pain, and the love in pain,
What I feared no longer consumed me,
I took control.

Family

I grew up close to my family,
Family get togethers
Birthday's
Living together
Sleepovers.
My grandparents gave me a huge family,
A family I adored,
Until everyone grew a part, became unavailable,
Some I don't even know,
Some I met once or twice.
I never understood why we all couldn't be close,
It seemed when we all grew,
We grew a part,
Some of my favorites, aren't anymore,
Some I don't care for, look right past in public, or
choose not to socialize with some at family events.
No one ever told me family would break,
I grew up loving them more,
I was taught family would stick together, but now, it's
like they only "stick together" because they feel they
need to, not because they love me as a person.
I don't have interest for some anymore,
I don't care if we share blood,
I have friends,
I have my man,
Who treat me more like family than blood.
Blood means relation, it doesn't mean love.

I won't fake it like I do, I wont love you just because
you're family,
I'm too honest to lie,
I'm too loyal to fake it.
Being family doesn't disregard your shitty personality,
Your fake energy,
Just like a friend, I can leave you behind,
Just like anyone, I don't need you.
So, don't ever use the family card on me,
Connections are the only thing important to me.

Tupac

A man that deserves to be forever celebrated,
An old soul,
A true inspiration,
I thank you,
For providing honesty in this tragic world,
For making the change you set out to,
Even though you didn't make the world change,
You opened my eyes,
You touched me.
The heart you had,
For the ones who didn't have it, the ones who didn't get
a chance,
You were never selfish
You were never prideful,
You braced your soul to the world without caring if it
would kill you,
The bravery, the honor,
A man like you, deserves to be remembered,
I will forever celebrate your soul.
I wish I was old enough in the era you lived,
I educate myself and learn you,
Your music, interviews, I listen.
One piece that spoke to me,
"My thought pattern is opposite of the norm,
So, I would have to change the world, or I'd have to be
changed by the world."
I felt the purpose.
No one told me standing up for myself could make me
an outcast, you taught me that.

I keep that line close to my heart,
I refuse to dim my light to help others shine,
I refuse to stay silence and not speak when it's time,
I fear how I'd be perceived,
They can't love me for everything I am, they don't
deserve to, at all.
Everyone's perception of me isn't a reflection of me,
It's a reflection of them,
I took that knowledge from you.
You taught me how to be brave,
You held no fear in your heart,
I strive to be that, I will be,
I won't settle for less,
I wont box myself into standards of anyone who can't
understand.
I will speak change through my words,
I will speak my truth,
I will make a difference,
I will keep being inspired.
A man of no greater thing,
But love and inspiration,
Thank you for being you,
Unapologetically you.

Self-love

There's something beautiful,
In loving myself wholeheartedly,
Through the struggles and insecurities,
Every day is a new battle,
Every day is a new triumph.

Grandparents

The tragedy of losing you both overpowers everything,
I try to recollect memories,
I'm faced trying to overcome the pain left with me from
losing you.
I was young,
I pushed the grief to the side,
I thought hiding from the pain meant it would
disappear.
Here I am,
10 years later,
Tears running down my face, I didn't know what it was
like to feel,
Now I'm forced to make peace with your absence.
Everyone always tells me,
"Write about your grandparents"
My mind always became clouded,
I chose to put it behind me,
In the dark part of my heart I let become cold,
Once upon a time.

Nana,
You were so beautiful,
Physically, soulfully, spiritually,
The love you expressed to everyone was inspiring,
No matter how you got treated in return,
Some of your children never came around until it was
too late,
You didn't deserve to be treated that way.

I grew up with you until I was 16,
You were a second mother to me,
I remember staying home from school sick watching
Pappy's Land with you,
I drew a picture, you mailed it in, the next episode my
drawing was on the TV,
You were so proud,
You always encouraged me to do anything I wanted.
You always helped me with homework.
There are missing pieces to this story, it hurts I can't
tell it all because I chose to push you away,
I didn't understand death,
The day you passed everyone was depressed,
I remember the looks and emotions in the room once
your soul left,
I was confused, but it broke my heart seeing my
mother lose you,
Which was my rejection to let any pain out the window,
But deep inside,
Seeing you without a beating heart, a cold hand, it
broke me.
I wish I could write all our memories,
It all comes back to how sick you were,
But the strength you held trying to show you weren't,
I have those same qualities,
I wish you were here to see my success.
I remember having a dream of you, years ago,
You were sitting in your rocking chair, after having
many dreams of you silently sitting there, you finally
spoke,
"I'm okay"
I haven't dreamt of you since,
I felt peace in that moment you came to me,

You knew it was hard for me even though I didn't show
it, you were patient with me.
My guardian angel,
You watch over me,
You're proud,
I know you're smiling,
I love you.

Poppy,
A man who had sass, I like to stay, a grumpy old man
who loved but never expressed with words,
Only with actions.
I'm thankful for how you took care of your wife,
50 years later,
You two are forever goals,
Not perfect, but the kind of love I'm happy I grew
around.
I remember you in your room always making boats,
planes, anything out of wood,
An artist you were, dedicated to finishing every piece,
I get that from you.
I remember,
Trips to take bubba to the doggy barber,
Trips to the grocery store, you always got the good
candy.
You were an introvert,
A smart man,
A great husband,
A great cook,
I miss you.
You weren't the kind to express much,
But the day before you passed you called me,
Asking why I didn't come visit you,

You told me you missed and loved me,
The next day you were gone.
I resented myself,
I was young,
I hated hospitals,
I didn't want to go, I thought you'd come home,
But you chose to leave before Nana,
You always said you didn't want to live without her.
I love you both so much,
If it's one thing I remember most,
The heart's you both had,
The heart I have for being loved by both,
What I took from you,
Life isn't the same without you,
Having you watch over me is peaceful,
I hope you're resting peacefully,
It's hell here sometimes,
The pain you both were in, is over,
I hated seeing you suffer.
I can now remember you for everything you passed
onto me,
I hope you're proud.

Shannon

You are my best friend in the universe,
Cousins by blood,
Best friends by life.
You taught me to be humble,
To always stay real.
We both share the same heart, I swear
I never have to ask for a thing,
I know you're always there,
And you know,
Without a request, I'm here.
Growing up you were always my idol,
A hardworking woman
Strong
Independent
Not perfect and lost her way sometimes,
Made some decisions that didn't stick,
To me that made you worthy of perfection,
The way you handled every situation,
With your heart of gold,
But also handled anyone who crossed you.
I never met anyone who didn't like you,
If they didn't, it wasn't anything you did.
An old soul not many understood,
You love hard,
One lesson I learned from you,
To walk away when you're not treated your worth,
To never feel worthless, instead,

Find that worth.
A strong woman you've always been,
I'm proud of you,
I'm happy to always be close when everyone in our
family became distant,
We grew together,
Even though our lives took different routes,
We understand life,
That alone makes our love remain strong.
A call,
Or drive away,
Nothing will ever change.

A true definition of a best friend
A true definition of love in pure form,
Thank you for being an inspiration,
All these years growing up without knowing I'd take a
piece of what you taught me,
There's no one I'd rather live up to, than you,
Keep being you.

Butterfly

I once had petty ways,
I once thought I should treat people
exactly how they treated me,
I was young
I was bitter
I was learning
I shouldn't be held hostage as the same I once was,
I grew.
In the eyes of one's I hurt, I didn't,
They remembered me for all the pain I brought,
They couldn't look passed,
Or see through,
I held myself accountable for all the times,
I brought pain,
Or was bitter,
I'm open, to admitting I wasn't proud of me,
I know I'm not perfection,
That's the thing,
I never wanted to be.
I don't regret a thing I've done,
I was,
Lost
Mistaken
Confused,
I took many shortcuts,
Which brought me down wrong paths.
I made decisions off fear,
I couldn't express myself,
I was a shy soul,

A soul who didn't understand the feeling of being whole.

I don't ask to be forgiven,
I don't ask to be given a second chance.
You don't need to see me as this magnificent soul who broke out her shell and grew,
I know some will never see it,
I never wanted to make sense to anyone,
I can own my past,
I can own my growth,
I transformed into this soul I'm proud of,
If you can't unseen the pain,
And see through,
You still have growing to do.

Letter to my Old Self

You were lost,
You were stuck in your own insecurities,
Which blocked you from blessings.
You never saw the beauty in you,
You searched for beauty in everyone else,
You chose to keep trying to find love in everyone else,
Yet couldn't come to terms with giving the same love to yourself.
You broke your own heart countless times,
You broke some good heart's,
They weren't "right"
You always chose wrong.
You projected your hurt onto anyone who tried to heal you, you let others try when you knew it wasn't their job,
You were wrong.
You stayed alone for years,
Wondering why no one would love you,
Why you weren't good enough,
Why no one could feel you.
You couldn't get it right,
You blamed your heart for all the times,
You chose to give it to the wrong people,
You always gave more than received,
You chased people who didn't want to be, you became out of breath when you realized.
All those years alone,
You could have filled yourself with the love,
Not waited until your late 20's.
You chose to find someone to always fill the void,

You hooked up with men,
Who couldn't give you what you needed,
You chose men,
Who were equally as damaged,
You thought fixing them meant they'd love you,
You were left to pick up your own pieces, theirs too.
You had terrible interest in men, friends too,
You let people walk all over you as you kept loving
them.
You let your "friends" disrespect you in the public,
While they "loved" you in private.
You let people try you without standing up for yourself,
I'm not saying you were right,
Because you weren't,
I'm not going to say sorry for all the bullshit,
I'm not.
The pain shaped you,
You were a lost soul,
I don't blame you for creating reckless behavior,
I don't blame you for damaging our heart,
I picked up the pieces and found our way.
I don't blame you for any of it,
I thank you for being a complete mess,
Without the lessons we wouldn't be living every
blessing.
You were learning, and loving, you just chose the
wrong ways of doing so, along with the wrong souls.
I can't be mad, look at us now,
Indestructible, invincible, and powerful.
Our souls are still searching, but became one,
We've found our home,
We're at peace,
It's okay, you can rest now.

Pushed Away

I pushed people away, good people,
I was hurt from the previous one,
They didn't deserve to hold my pain,
Or try and save me,
They weren't a superhero,
With love powers that could heal any soul,
But I put the pressure on them,
I took the rage I had, out on them like it was their
disaster.
I wasn't healed, I was damaged,
To try and love another,
Without being over the last,
Wishing to have that old thing back,
They didn't deserve to walk into the mess my heart was
left with,
They didn't deserve to love that side of me.
I wasn't over what I was left with to pick up from my
own mistakes, to keep loving someone who proved
they didn't love me back.
It was my fault I held on when they cut ties.
I don't know why I felt the need to prove my love,
It wouldn't have gone this far if I saw the light,
I projected my pain onto good people,
Ones who may have been good for me,
I wasn't good to them.
I pray they found someone to love them, I couldn't,
I couldn't even love myself,
I hope they felt that.

Friend Zoned

High school love,
I did everything to show I wanted them,
They did everything to show me they didn't.
Years later,
Wanted a chance,
Far too late,
Sorry for our timelines,
They never matched our hearts.

"Supporting Someone You Love Even Though It Hurts"

I remember being patient,
Trying to make sense of something you never opened
your eyes to.
I remember being there,
When you needed a shoulder,
Or a few words of encouragement to help you.
I remember when you told me all the reasons to go,
But always chose to stay.
I remember listening to you repeat,
You couldn't stand for the disrespect,
The trust died long ago,
But you continued to fight,
For a love that was only felt within you,
More than it was ever reciprocated back to you.
He loved you,
Just not enough as you wanted of him.
I watched you be unhappy,
While you preached to the world how happy you were,
I felt you when you spoke those painful moments,
I heard you,
The problem was,
You couldn't.
I watched you chose a fate that clearly wasn't meant to
stick, only meant to cross.
The universe presented a sign,
I couldn't support your continuous on loving someone,
Who's road is trying to reach another destination.

You believed in making things work, so you tried.
You spoke a lot in private,
That never matched what was presented to the public,
The negativity grew,
You were unhappy with you,
It reflected onto us,
I couldn't support your decision to stay,
While leaving you behind,
To cater to someone who couldn't love you the way you
needed, I knew,
But you chose to stay,
So, I chose to go.
We didn't see eye to eye when it came to love,
You loved through it all,
I loved until I couldn't anymore,
I knew when it was time to walk away,
You couldn't imagine starting over.
You were comfortable in your unhappiness,
You placed your hatred onto me,
Because I saw through the love you fought for,
The love you believed was true.
One thing we didn't agree on,
Threw you off the edge.
As I picked up different pieces of myself,
The more I lost of you,
You only shaped me,
For all the things I didn't want.

Love at First Sight

We met months before,
Facetimed,
The moment we met at that red light,
I looked over to my right,
Saw you on the sidewalk looking back at me,
I felt the feeling rush through my body,
I felt all the doubt I had about love,
Leaving my body.
I knew right then,
This was going to be it.
I loved you at first sight,
In that moment,
I knew you loved me too.

A Decade of Friendship

A best friend,
Who turned into a sister,
It amazes me,
How strong our love is,
Through the many years we spent a part,
For no reason at all,
But life.
We can always pick up where we left off,
Like we didn't spend time apart,
It amazes me,
How we stayed close,
Through our differences,
We always grew together,
Accepted each other for who we are,
Loving each other for everything we are,
That's why we're no longer best friends,
We're sisters.
There's something special about a friend who doesn't
try and change you,
That's why I know without a doubt,
We're in this until forever.

Twin Souls

My soul has matched with many souls,
Many haven't stayed,
It was years residing,
Or a quick imprint on my heart and leave,
My soul connected,
Twin souls,
Not meant to live with the life God destined for me.
If I couldn't grow with them,
I outgrew them first,
I couldn't hold on and keep fighting,
Love isn't war,
My love was for the sacred,
No one who is present now,
Was meant to be close until God calls me home,
I've made peace with soulmates,
Teaching their lessons,
To leave when it's time,
I was bitter at first,
The thought of losing a soulmate was tragic,
Not everyone touched that place in my heart was
meant to stay,
Some came and went after years of learning and
loving.
My intuition tried to tell me it wasn't forever,
That's why I was bitter.
I didn't feel I did what I should have to keep them,
Until I woke and saw,
Love isn't a game,
You don't win or lose.
Love is an emotion,

Something you feel,
Not something you can choose.
I overlooked the times I was blind to what love was,
Because the illusion I placed on it.

Soulmates came,
They went,
My heart hurt,
How could I lose a love after I gave them everything,
Without leaving a piece for me.
Twin souls,
I found many in this lifetime,
We went together until we didn't,
The road spilt,
We both hit closure,
Trying to find each other again,
It wasn't in the cards,
Our love,
Was only meant to be a lesson,
A memory.
A moment in time,
We once were.
A love I'll never forget,
It made me love harder,
It made me wiser,
It made me stronger.
I can let go without dying inside,
I still love them,
For everything they brought to my life,
The peace I found in their absence,
Has brought the kind of bliss loving them never did.

Let's Talk About Sex

I had several hook ups,
Meaningless sex was fun until it was time to lay down
at night, all alone.
My mind became a dangerous place,
I yearned for love,
Becoming victim of giving myself to men,
Who didn't want more,
So, I thought, a little fun might hold over the thought of
love visiting.
I thought love may come from a broken soul,
I was wrong.
Sex was fun in the moment,
Until I came to wanting to held at night,
Or for the rest of my life.
Someone who was a hopeless romantic,
I saw the good in everyone,
I thought I had the power of bringing out the good in
everyone,
I thought I could create love where it wasn't desired,
I thought my love hit different.
I was tire of trying to be woke to someone who couldn't
understand my language of love,
I became victim of my own heart break,
As I laid down with men,
I knew wouldn't give me what I needed,
I just always yearned for what I didn't have,
Until I met someone who was 1,200 miles away,
The kind of passion,
My heart exploded without a touch,
Without a single sexual desire,

Turning into someone more powerful.
I yearned to be close,
I yearned to feel his touch.
I flew cross the coast to see if what I felt was real,
It couldn't be ignored,
The passion was powerful.
The moment we met,
We locked eyes and it was over.
We knew it was us.
I felt safe,
I felt my whole life change,
My soul felt at home,
I felt what it's like to make love,
It was more than those meaningless hook ups,
I tried to turn into love,
The direction I took got me lost.
A passion that's never been opened before,
The love we share is out this world,
I swear we met on the moon in our past life,
Because our hearts knew,
This passion,
The love we share,
It's too powerful to explain,
But damn.

Different Kinds of Love

I loved someone with almost all of me,
I couldn't give them all,
I didn't yet love all of me.
I loved deeply for someone,
Who almost broke me,
I found myself picking up the pieces,
Trying to put them back together,
To fill a void that was vacant.
I was never broken, I'm still here,
There were missing pieces in my story,
I grew without,
I was searching,
I tried making pieces fit that shouldn't.
I gave my open heart, open arms to someone who used
me to place their insecurities onto me,
To break me so I could be the lost one,
I ended up forgotten in my own mind,
I lost every memory of happiness trying to fill their
void.
I gave until I couldn't fill them anymore,
What I once could, wasn't possible anymore,
I couldn't create something that wasn't there,
I'm not a magician,
I couldn't make love appear, or be felt,
So, we just searched for a void to fill in each other like
a broken world,
Trying to love together,
Trust issues

Insecurities
Scars,
In a world filled with souls who wander but never find
the love they crave,
The simple act of attention fills the void for a second,
So, they forget,
Until their heart cries again.
I loved everyone who made me feel something,
I still hold love for you,
Doesn't mean I want you, or need you,
The love once felt reached its limit,
I always had a void with you,
One you couldn't fill,
You weren't bad,
Or couldn't give someone what you tried to give me,
It just couldn't be,
You weren't right for me,
I needed a little extra.
When I couldn't write how beautiful it was,
I bottled myself up,
I knew I was burning away my soul,
You were toxic to me because I forced it,
I became toxic to myself when I believed you,
I held the words I love you close,
Until it came to choosing between love and you,
You didn't make my heart skip a special beat,
The love you made me feel,
Was mediocre,
Compared to the love I found after you.

"Toxic people,
Have a way of making you believe you're wrong,
The scariest part,
You become toxic to yourself by believing them."

Emotionally Abused

Physically drained,
Emotionally abused,
Believing you card enough to let me go without leaving
me bruised.
Many told me "love hurts"
You just need to make it through,
Love isn't perfect, they said,
You need to constantly work,
Troubles may arise,
You'll feel the need to work overtime to breakthrough,
Work for it, Work at it,
I think that's why I always chased it,
I thought I could save it, or anyone I placed the illusion
upon.
I blame myself for the rush I placed on finding love,
I worked overtime trying to prove my heart.
The constant distance that held us a part,
Being together so much,
I couldn't soak in the regret of feeling I didn't do
enough.
God gave me a heart,
Why would I turn cold and disown the gift?
My vulnerability scared you,
You wanted me to love you on your terms,
I was a prize to you,
I was lost within the self you made of me,
I lost all sight of what I loved,
I was blind the toxicity of us,

Until I broke free.
I found happiness in people,
Ones who let me be free,
Without trying to change me,
While you threw dirt on my name,
Because "I hurt you"
Only because it was public,
And your dirt was behind closed doors,
You became victim when seeing what it cost.
I wasn't ever a priority,
I wasn't ever a need,
I was a fix,
A temporary lover,
The love I couldn't give,
I loved hard,
Emotions scared you,
You tried to dim my love to your liking,
We crashed.
I couldn't catch a break trying to please you,
I couldn't be free and fly,
You broke my wings,
You convinced me you were it.
I didn't let you intoxicate me with your language of
love,
A love I was accustomed to,
A love I was comfortable with,
I never felt anything good before you,
So, I held on,
Years spent unhappy,
Having to silence my heart for you,
I guess that's why when I left,
I never felt a thing.

Seasons

I live with the four seasons,
I can't stand change,
But here,
It's constant,
Spring
Spring
Summer
Fall
Winter,
Repeat.
Four seasons of changes,
I sometimes wish time could stop and stay in summer,
Beach nights under the moonlight,
Speaking life into existence,
Clear, sun kissed skin,
No seasonal depression in sight,
I'm happy,
Life seems whole,
Until it's cold and lifeless,
I'm a summer baby,
But I've grown to appreciate the changes,
I appreciate life.

Ocean

I like to think of our love as the ocean,
There may be waves,
They're calming,
There's no telling if it ends.

Single

Being single was my motto for years,
Not by choice, more so, by default.
I wanted to be loved,
But also, barricaded my heart behind this wall.
I was always the single friend,
The third wheel,
Witnessing the love,
But also, the heartache,
A front row seat to everything I should have,
It made it harder to find someone worthy.
I attracted the impacted more than the founded,
I was a mess,
An open book,
I was read many times,
No one had what it took to read the whole thing,
No one took the time to learn me.
No one ever got it all,
In both heart and intimate ways,
There was always a wall,
There was always something missing,
Something I was holding back,
Sometimes I was always angry about,
A constant war I fought with myself.
The single girl,
Who always had someone to talk to,
Because I was searching for something in someone,
I thought I lost or had to find,
I was trying hard not to be single,
I thought single meant lonely,
I thought I needed someone to fulfill me.

Living in Tension Between Desires and Commitments

The living tension of working 9-5,
Listening to miserable people spread their negativity,
While I give them a smile and show respect,
They still attack me without my control,
I always wondered,
Does it get tiring to project that kind of hate?
A question I won't ever get answered,
I can wear a fake smile perfectly,
And speak with the highest amount of respect,
Yet, get walked over because they're always right,
That's how it works right?
Whether the time I worked retail or medical,
Everyone treats the worker with the least respect,
Why, because we deserve it?
We have all worked,
We know how it feels to be an overworked soul,
Without the pay we deserve,
To put up with much more work than we signed up for,
They expect us to be happy,
My heart cries as I die inside,
From the misery of working that 9-5 I can only stand
for a short amount of time,
Until someone destroy my ay with one thing they say.
I get everyone has a problem that aren't known by the
public, we all carry something with us closely.
We don't speak, so we erupt without realizing,
It's hurtful to project your problems onto another,
If I'm being nice to you, please be kind.

I'm sorry you're going through something,
How do you know I'm not struggling too?
The tension of living in a world full of disrespectful
soul's who don't care about another,
The commitment of waking up everyday at 7:30 to be to
work for 8,
As I wait until I clock out,
The anxiety of having to do another day of the misery,
The desire of creating at any time of the day is ruined,
My mind is flooded by the remarks from people I don't
know,
Trying to stay positive while working amongst
negativity.
It's hard being an artist working a 9-5,
Being treated less of who I am,
Working for a job that doesn't acknowledge my worth,
Bills need to be paid,
So, I stick to my commitments,
As I pray,
I can make It through this world we live in,
I feel like I've been to hell almost every day,
Until I clock out and write.
The tension placed between my desires and
commitments,
I only pray one day I can make a living off what I
desire,
Until then,
The tension of living in hell,
Until I make it to heaven.

Regret

I hold no regrets,
I hold no repeated pain in vain,
I chose not to soak in it,
I chose to live in it,
Make my way through it.
I couldn't heal.
If I kept putting the weight and blame on my heart.

Forgiveness

It's easy to say sorry,
Unless of course,
Pride,
But for I,
I had no problem saying sorry,
I meant it,
I was honest with my decisions,
I never fooled anyone, but I.
I forgave a lot of ones who almost broke me,
I forgave when I shouldn't have.
Forgiveness is easy,
When you're honest,
When you're someone of ego it's hard,
It's a weak act, some say.
Forgiving is more for me than you,
To set myself free of the burden,
To set myself free of everything slowly killing me.
Forgiveness is a power most fear,
Forgiveness will set you free,
If you're ever faced with the decision,
Forgiveness heals,
Start there.

I remember feeling broken after breakups, mainly because I chose to give more than I demanded in return, so it resulted in my own heart break. In reality, I was never broken, I was lost. I know now, I never experienced real heart break until the day I lost you. The heartbreak of losing you gave me a rush of anxiety and complete utter sadness I didn't think I would have come back from. I wanted you near, I wanted you to be whole. I wanted you to be with everyone who loved you. I was broken for their heart's too. I remember crying and trying to find answers without understanding I wasn't going to find one. I felt alone trying to heal from the heartache as I struggled to get through with my writing, that's how I speak to you, or finding myself under the moon, that's where I always felt you. I spent a year trying to grieve in the darkness of people telling me "I'm sorry you lost her, but I can be your friend", people didn't understand how it felt to have your heart ripped out their chest and not yet reached its destination back. I found it cruel no one understood my pain, it was written all over me. I felt the pain everyday as I tried desperately to hide behind the smile I gave, I became good at pretending. I found myself bursting into tears trying to understand how it was possible. I lived a whole year lost, a whole year trying to understand the vacant part of my soul that needed your presence. It is two years since you left, and one year since my first book release I did in your honor, I'm so proud, I hope you are too, of my accomplishments, and for my broken heart that's mended, the piece you took, realizing it's possible to go on without, I don't need it, it's yours.

I no longer like the term "sorry for your loss" because your spirit and soul still live on, I feel you everywhere I go, you make it, so I know you never left. It was a long road of being confused, I prayed a lot to have you back, instead, I got waking up every morning at 3 a.m. to the moon shining through my window. A cute blue orb in all of pictures of the moon. You brought the love of my life the time I needed him most. The inspiration of finding myself through all the madness, everything that transitioned after your passing was dull until you came and brought all the light I needed. To have aa guardian angel as beautiful as you, I'm blessed and incredibly thankful to have known you, to have loved you, to have felt you. I continue to hold you close to my heart. I don't search for anything unless it's within myself, to make myself the best version of myself, you taught me how important that is. I will forever live to prove the inspiration you flow through me. You will always be apart of me Josie. We are one now. I miss you, but I'm happy you're near. Thank you for showing me what real friendship is.

"The love I have to give is intense,
But intensely beautiful,
There's nothing I wouldn't do for you,
If I love you,
That's the way my heart is set up,
It will always go the length of proving how deep
my love goes,
Without taking the love I have for myself away."

"My soul craves a different kind of love,
The kind you give me,
The spontaneous,
Welcome home kind of love,
A love I never felt before,
A love greater than any kind I experienced,
Your love is security,
Your love is special."

Dreams

Vivid dreams scare me,
I always think,
Are they trying to tell me something?
I dreamt about my best friend of 7 years,
Who I'm no longer friends with,
Because I chose to ghost her,
I couldn't deal with the constant competition we had going,
I didn't realize I was a part of,
Until I woke up from the dream.
I was bitter for so long,
I didn't take the time to see how I became consumed,
Our friendship started in 2010,
Juniors in high school,
Different schools but held strong,
Sleepovers
Parties
Long talks
Graduating college
Having children,
I was there for her happiest moments,
The ones she was most proud,
I thought that's what mattered most,
Until our friendship took a turn,
When I started my own life,
Our lives started growing in different directions,
I was living life,
She was growing as a mother,
We both worked different hours,

We let life get between us,
It caused us to break.
We tried to stay strong the many times life came and
blew through,
We stayed strong through the hurricane,
Which ended up a disaster.
I don't know when our lives became a competition,
I don't know when our friendship lost direction,
We lost all signs of love we felt,
We spilt many times,
The big moments brought us back together,
The time my friend passed,
I made it my mission to let her know I would be
devasted without her,
I needed to express my love.
The time her boyfriend stepped out on her,
She came to me because I was right about her friend.
We loved each other,
It became toxic,
We didn't keep it healthy.
The burdens we held which made us happy,
We took out on each other.
I was tired of being her muse for pain,
Put my heart in overtime to try and make her see me,
I lived to prove myself,
While she put me down.
We were both unable to give each other the love we
wanted to each other,
We struggled to give that love to ourselves.
It's been 2 years since we spoke,
My heart still loves her,
Many memories attached to forget,
Everything we grew,

Our friendship broke me,
Our friendship helped me grow.
We went through pain, love and much toxicity,
I couldn't hold on any longer,
I let go.
I had this dream,
Of the present year,
Seeing her after 2 years,
We rekindled things,
I remember her whispering in my ear,
"I'm desperate to get out"
I woke up,
Anxious to know if she's okay,
If she's thinking of me too.
God had brought us back together many times,
This time she's out of reach,
I couldn't find a way to get in touch,
So, I'm praying for her,
Praying she's not unhappy.
After all this time,
I'm not bitter,
I want her to be happy,
It breaks my heart not being able to reach her,
But I left it in God's hands,
If it's meant to be,
He'll make a way,
If not, he'll project her,
I just wish she knew,
I'm sorry,
And my love is as strong as ever.

"you're entitled to your own opinion,
But please,
Keep it to yourself,
My life is off limits."

*"I'm a butterfly,
Breaking free from the cocoon I was placed in.*

*I'm the mystery of the moon at night,
But sheds light on so many."*

"Whether it's someone I know,
Or just met,
I'm always in tune with my intuition,
I pay attention to the energy you present to me,
Along with your language of communication.
Your vibe is a language that doesn't lie.
So, don't blame me if I don't choose you."

Self-Inflicting Toxic Behavior

I never saw anything wrong with my actions,
I always gave my heart to the ones I loved,
Even if it meant taking more of me,
To help heal them.
I took more than I could manage,
I became lost in them,
I forgot to hold myself strong,
I didn't think their burdens would make me crash,
I thought I was giving a helping hand,
Instead,
I gave my heart as tribute,
I became toxic to my own need,
I became overwhelmed being their need,
I was so accustomed,
I didn't know my meaning,
I thought saving people was my calling,
Until it was my turn to be saved,
No one was there,
I was left in this cold dark place,
Far from the soul I was,
My heart kept beating but I lost control of the direction,
It was known for giving, loving, and protecting
everyone else,
It didn't know how to give the same energy back to me.
I spent so much time worrying about everyone else,
I forgot to love myself,
I didn't know how to,
My flaws got the best of me,

My heart was big,
I still believed I wasn't enough.
I became toxic to myself,
When I damaged myself for their need.
I became toxic to myself,
When I hurt good people for the ones who wronged me.
I became toxic to myself,
When I believed the lies and overlooked the signs.
I let go of everyone who couldn't understand I had to work on myself,
I had to love myself,
It was the most challenging thing,
To watch one's I loved for so long go,
As it benefited me, I just didn't know.
Once I acknowledged they weren't the only one who brought the poison,
That I, was the most damaging.
Everyone has wake up call,
Mine was on time,
I don't regret a thing because I'm ready to love,
If anytime they wanted to start over,
I'm ready,
This time I know better,
This time I know what I have to offer.

Michael

In love with you more every day,
Growing in love is a different kind of love.

Promise

I promise to always take care of I,
So, I can take care of you.

I promise to never let my weakness, moodiness,
Come between us, instead, come to an understanding.

I promise to always be true to us.
I promise to always give us the same effort I give
myself.

I promise to love you with every part of my being,
Until the day I can no longer breathe.

I promise.

Healing from Someone You Still Love

I'm sorry it came down to which was more important, trying to make you love me, or saving my entire being from becoming lost. I'm sorry for leaving you when I promised I never would. I'm sorry I broke so many promises. I'm sorry my growth scared you, and your eyes saw it as change. I'm sorry you couldn't understand the difference but always wanted different. I'm sorry you didn't love yourself the way you wanted, so you chose to use my heart for your burdens. I'm sorry you saw me as someone who could be without you, so you chose to push me in that direction. I'm sorry you couldn't find who you were, so you created who you wanted to be and in the end you never felt whole. I'm sorry I couldn't love you the way you hoped I could. I'm sorry you demanded so much, but never thought what I gave was enough. I'm sorry I couldn't be the friend you wanted me to be. I'm sorry I need to love you from afar. I'm sorry the love we once shared became toxic to us. I'm sorry my soul won't ever get to rest without you. I'm sorry I loved you even when you didn't deserve it. I'm sorry I still do. Healing from someone you still love, it's crazy, after all this time, there's always love in my heart for you. But when I noticed your absence brought me peace, I knew one thing for sure, I wasn't sorry for choosing me.

"Don't ever go against your intuition,
It always steers you in the right direction."

"It's impossible to love someone who's intoxicated by someone before you, I've been there, I received love, but only under their conditions of what love is. To fully love, without your past haunting you, you'll need to let go of all the burden chasing you from that lost love."

2019

I had nothing to complain about,
You were good to me.
I'm alive,
I'm healthy.
There were moments that brought me low,
But the strength I've gained over the years brought a
different perspective.
A year of more growth, happiness, and love.
I'm blessed.

Josephine

I can't forget the pain I feel when it comes to remembering the loss of you. I can't forget the depression I was stuck in trying to make sense of your passing. I cried endless tears. I did everything I could to feel close to you again. I reminisced memories of us. I thought of my favorite moments, only to be sunk deeper into my anxious nerves. I was forced to understand death. I was forced to feel. I couldn't comprehend why you were placed into my life just to pass through so soon. I tried to put piece together that didn't fit, just to find an answer. I prayed every night to get a sign from you. I prayed every night to somehow heal from the pain of losing you. I felt alone as no one around me knew you, the one's who did, they didn't feel you like I did. I went to therapy. I talked about you to someone I didn't know, as if it would help me heal, I thought maybe they could bring some insight on what I felt was missing. As time passed, I lost connections with people I loved for almost decades, to people I loved for years. The signs started presenting, they weren't hard to notice, they were so clear. I remember every little sign. I remember every feeling I've felt when you presented your soul to me in spirit form. I remember praying for you to come back. I remember being helpless, not thinking I would ever make it through. I remember wishing it was all a nightmare, and I'd wake up and you'd be here. I didn't think it was possible, the amount of tears I cried. I didn't think it was possible, the amount of loneliness I felt, grieving over you without the shoulder of anyone that could remotely feel me. It was a roller-coaster of emotions you left me with. I succumbed every battle I thought I'd lost, I made it through with the help of you.

Loneliness felt less when you touched my soul. To wish to have you back, but to be in touch with your afterlife soul, a beautiful miracle I've witnessed. You have brought the brightest light into my life, while taking out the darkest parts that kept me down. My life has little mishaps since you've been my angel, everything is aligning how you knew I deserved. I know it's all because of you, it's been nothing but miracles since you've made sense of your departure. I was once bitter, angry, and confused. You brought my life a new sense of understanding and purpose. I no longer look at death and see sadness, I know it's going to hurt, it's going to take time, but what I'll always remember, is no matter what you showed me while living, you also showed me afterlife. Your soul keeps shining. My beautiful moon, I always search for you in the night, as you shine bright through my window. I didn't know what a true friend was until I met you. The most important lesson in life you taught me, was to love and let go, and even after letting go, you can still love.

The End

Before you go, I want to thank you for reading every page. If you've read my other books, you will see my growth in these pages. I hope you felt each piece, if you could relate, and if not, I hope you could feel my journey. I'm not someone who writes to be relatable, I write exactly how I feel, if you stumble across something that matches you, that's beautiful. Many might not connect with many of these pieces due to personal experiences and very personal stories shared, but I wanted to change the reading process, I wanted you to read this from my view, not yours.

Thank you again,
Yours truly,
Moonsoulchild

My Other Books:

The Journey Through My Heart
I Was Never Broken
Letters To You
The Journey Through My Heart: Part II
Dear Anonymous
Heal Inspire Love: Affirmations for the soul
The Soul Collection of Moonsoulchild

Social Media:

Instagram: @Moonsoulchild
Twitter: @Moonssoulchild
Facebook: Moonsoulchild

Made in the USA
Columbia, SC
30 April 2021

37160276R00102